I0799757

NATURAL DISASTERS Where I Live

EARTHQUAKES

Tracy Vonder Brink

A Stingray Book

SEAHORSE PUBLISHING

Teaching Tips for Caregivers and Teachers:

This Hi-Lo book features high-interest subject matter that will appeal to all readers in intermediate and middle school grades. It may be enjoyed by students reading at or above grade level as well as by those who are looking for age-appropriate themes matched with a less challenging reading level. Hi-Lo books are ideal for ELL readers, too.

Each book appeals to a striving reader's age and maturity level. Opportunities are provided for students to read words they already know while encountering a limited number of new, high-interest vocabulary words. With these supports in place, students will read more fluently while increasing reading comprehension. Use the following suggestions to help students grow as readers.

- Encourage the student to read independently at home.
- Encourage the student to practice reading aloud.
- Encourage activities that require reading.
- Establish a regular reading time.
- Have the student write questions about what they read.

Teaching Tips for Teachers:

Before Reading

- Ask, "What do I know about this topic?"
- Ask, "What do I want to learn about this topic?"

During Reading

- Ask, "What is the author trying to teach me?"
- Ask, "How is this like something I already know?"

After Reading

- Discuss how the text features (headings, index, etc.) help with understanding the topic.
- Ask, "What interesting or fun fact did you learn?"

TABLE OF CONTENTS

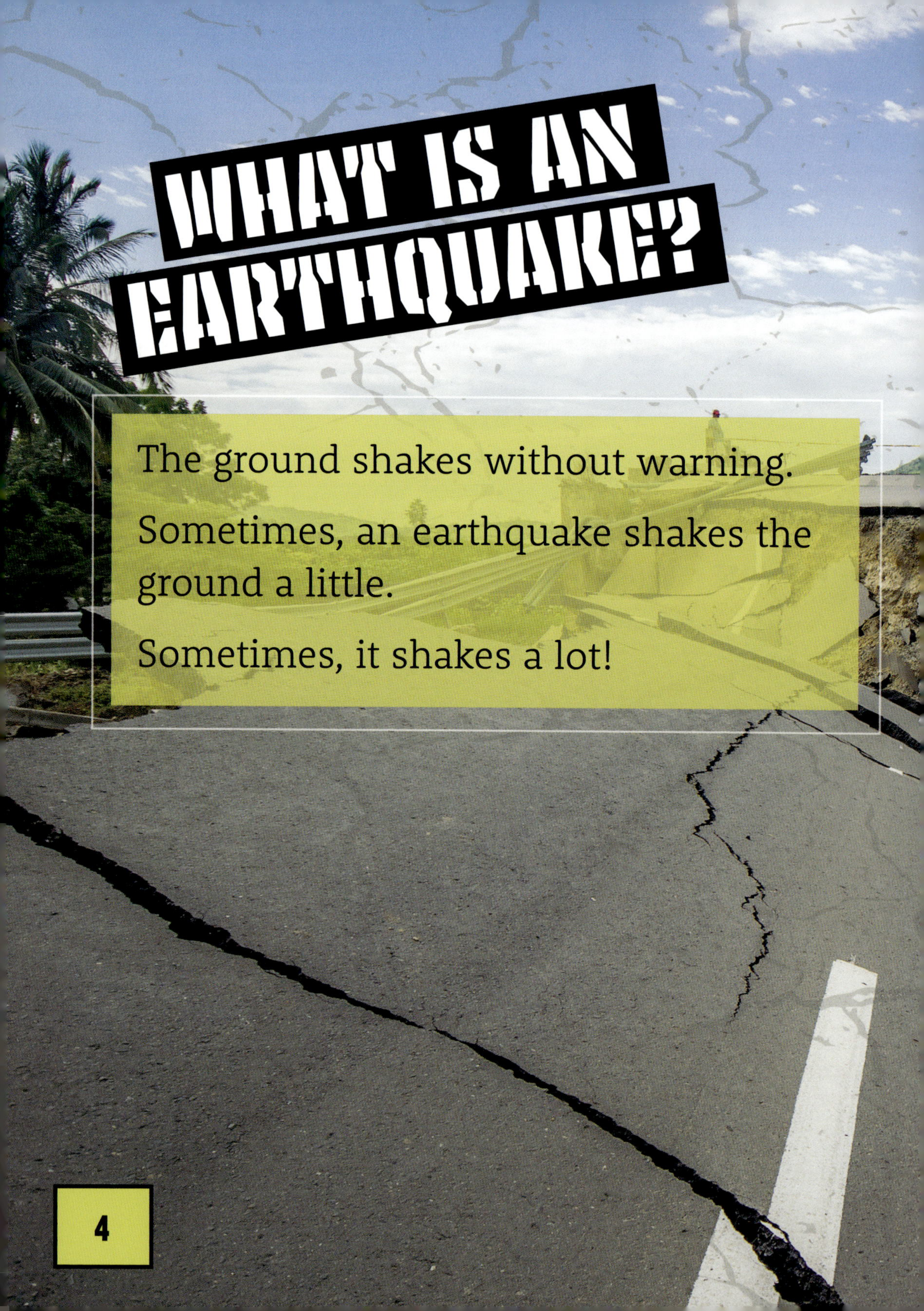

WHAT IS AN EARTHQUAKE?

The ground shakes without warning.

Sometimes, an earthquake shakes the ground a little.

Sometimes, it shakes a lot!

QUAKE FACT

Earthquakes cause the most damage in cities. They can shatter windows, topple buildings, break underground pipes, and destroy roads.

EARTH'S SURFACE

Earth has many layers. The **crust** is the top layer.

The crust is made up of separate pieces called **plates**. The plates fit together like the pieces of a puzzle.

The plates are always moving. But they move so slowly that we usually can't feel it.

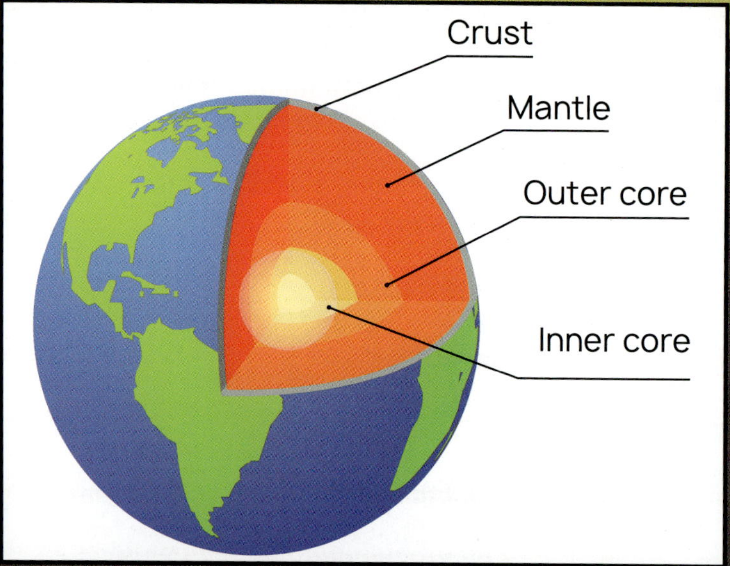

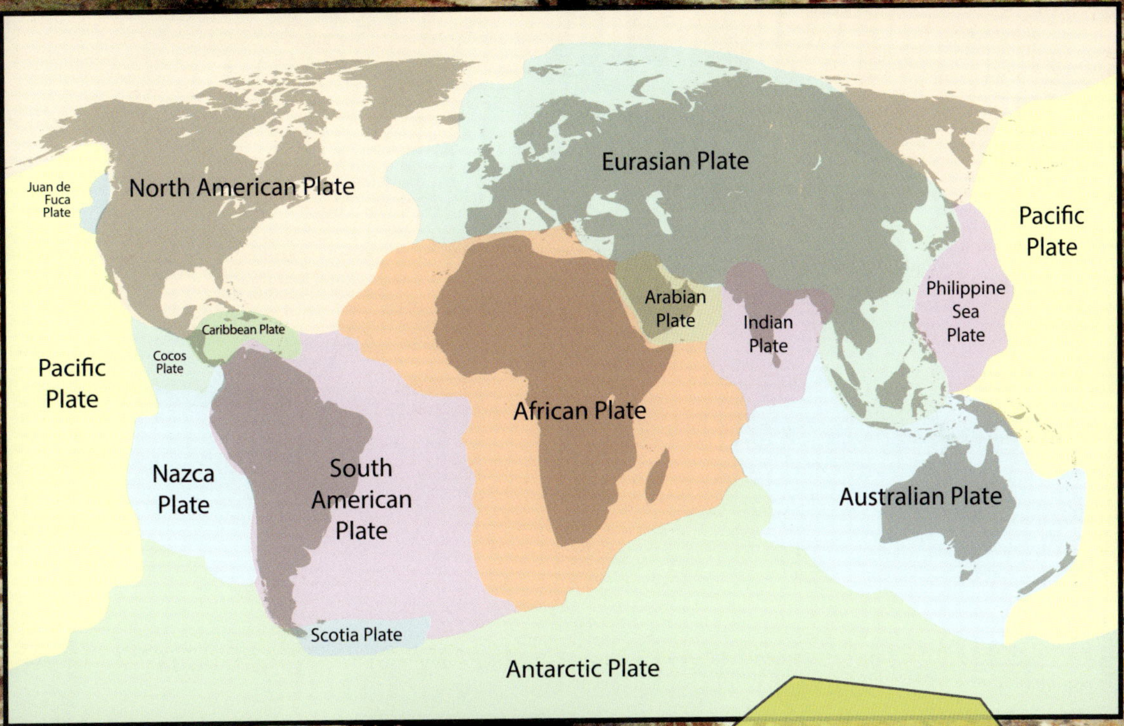

QUAKE FACT

Earth's plates move about one to two inches (three to five centimeters) per year. That's slower than your fingernails grow.

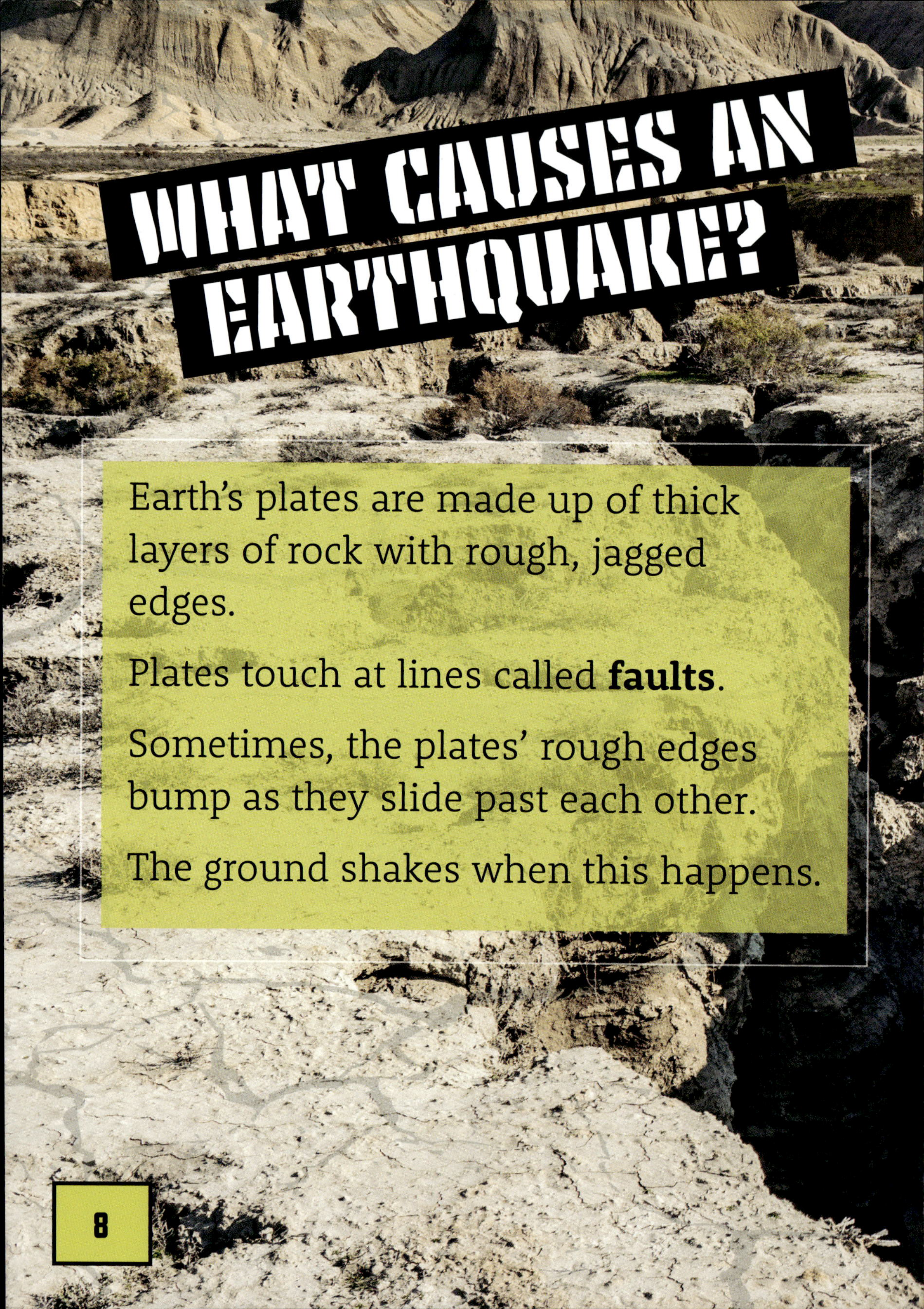

WHAT CAUSES AN EARTHQUAKE?

Earth's plates are made up of thick layers of rock with rough, jagged edges.

Plates touch at lines called **faults**.

Sometimes, the plates' rough edges bump as they slide past each other.

The ground shakes when this happens.

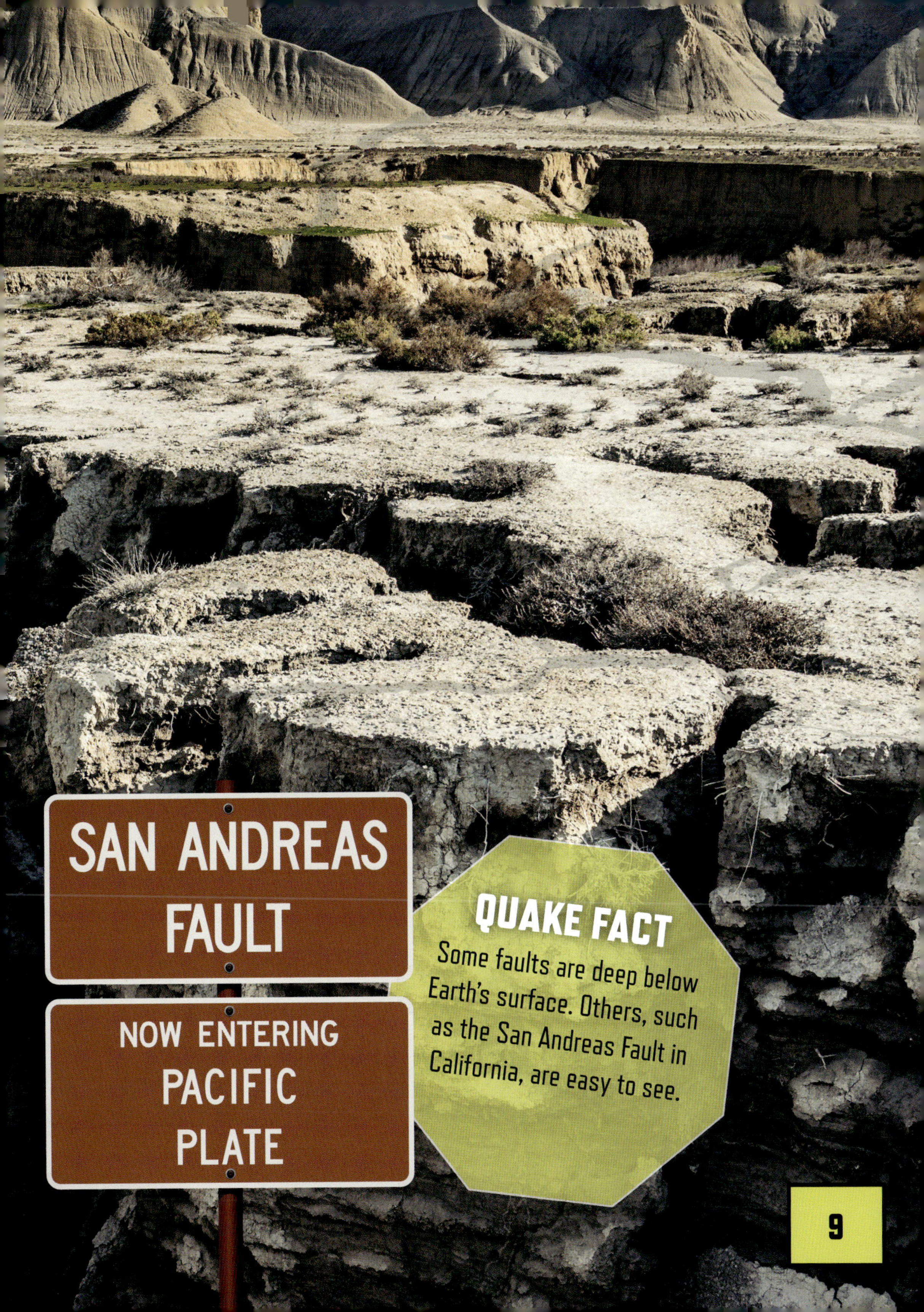

QUAKE FACT

Some faults are deep below Earth's surface. Others, such as the San Andreas Fault in California, are easy to see.

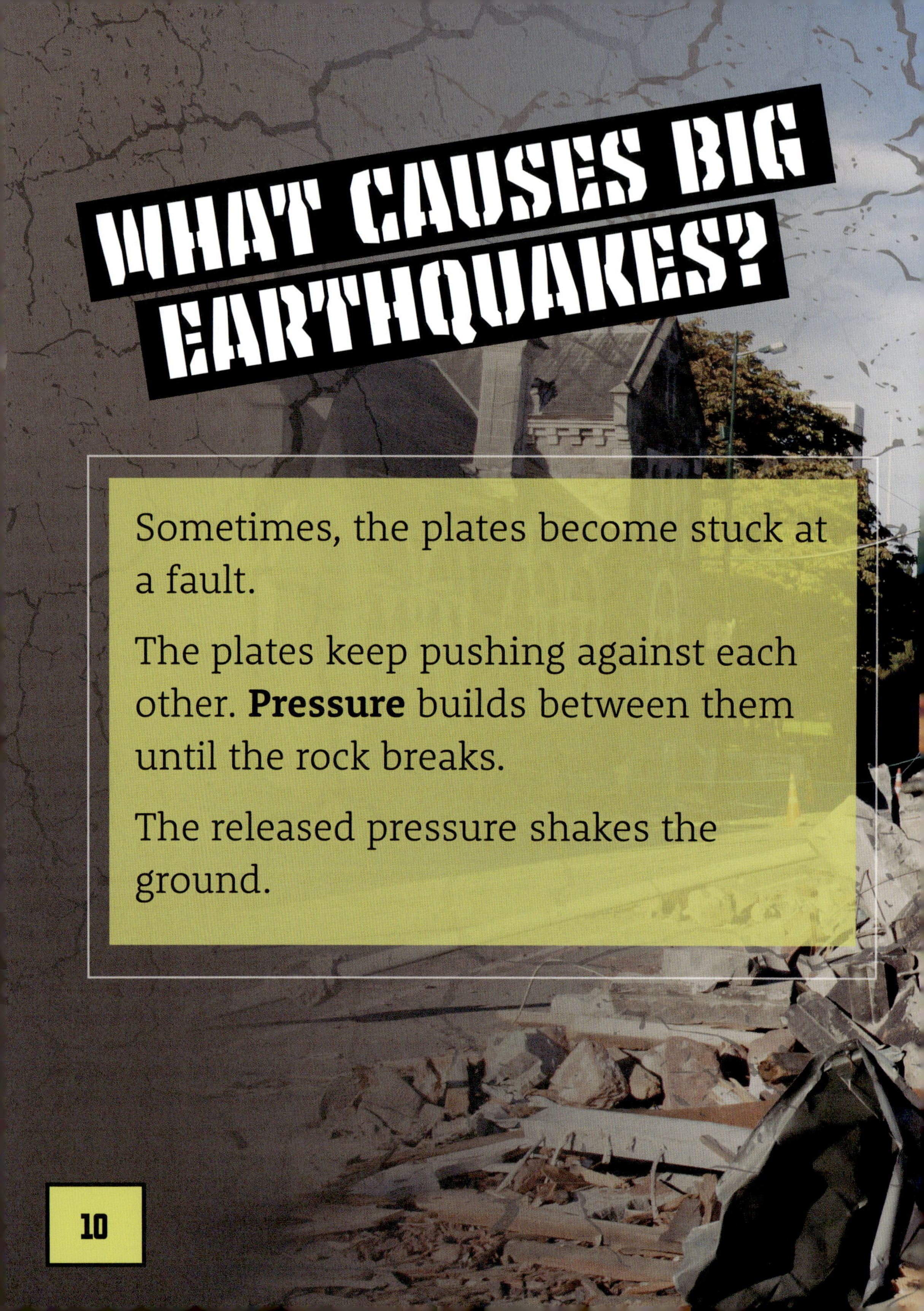

WHAT CAUSES BIG EARTHQUAKES?

Sometimes, the plates become stuck at a fault.

The plates keep pushing against each other. **Pressure** builds between them until the rock breaks.

The released pressure shakes the ground.

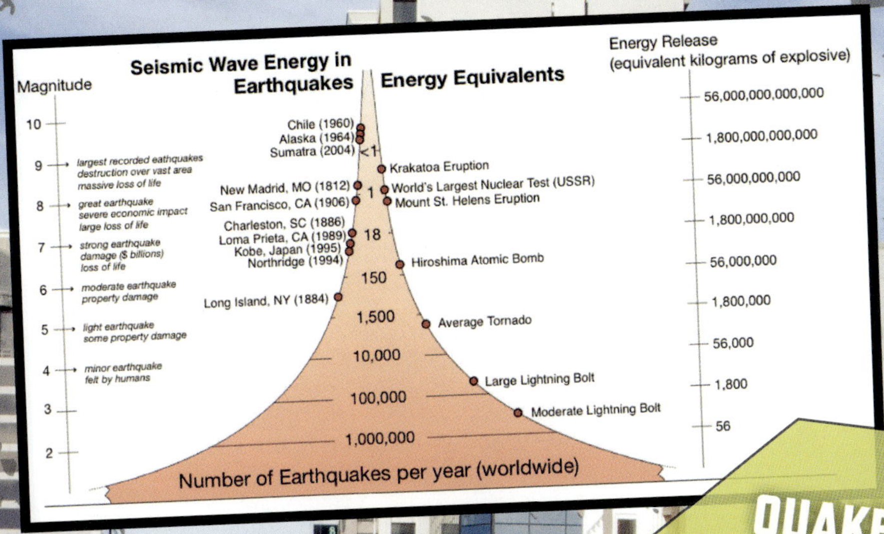

QUAKE FACT

Large earthquakes are measured using the Moment Magnitude Scale. It shows how much total energy was released during the earthquake.

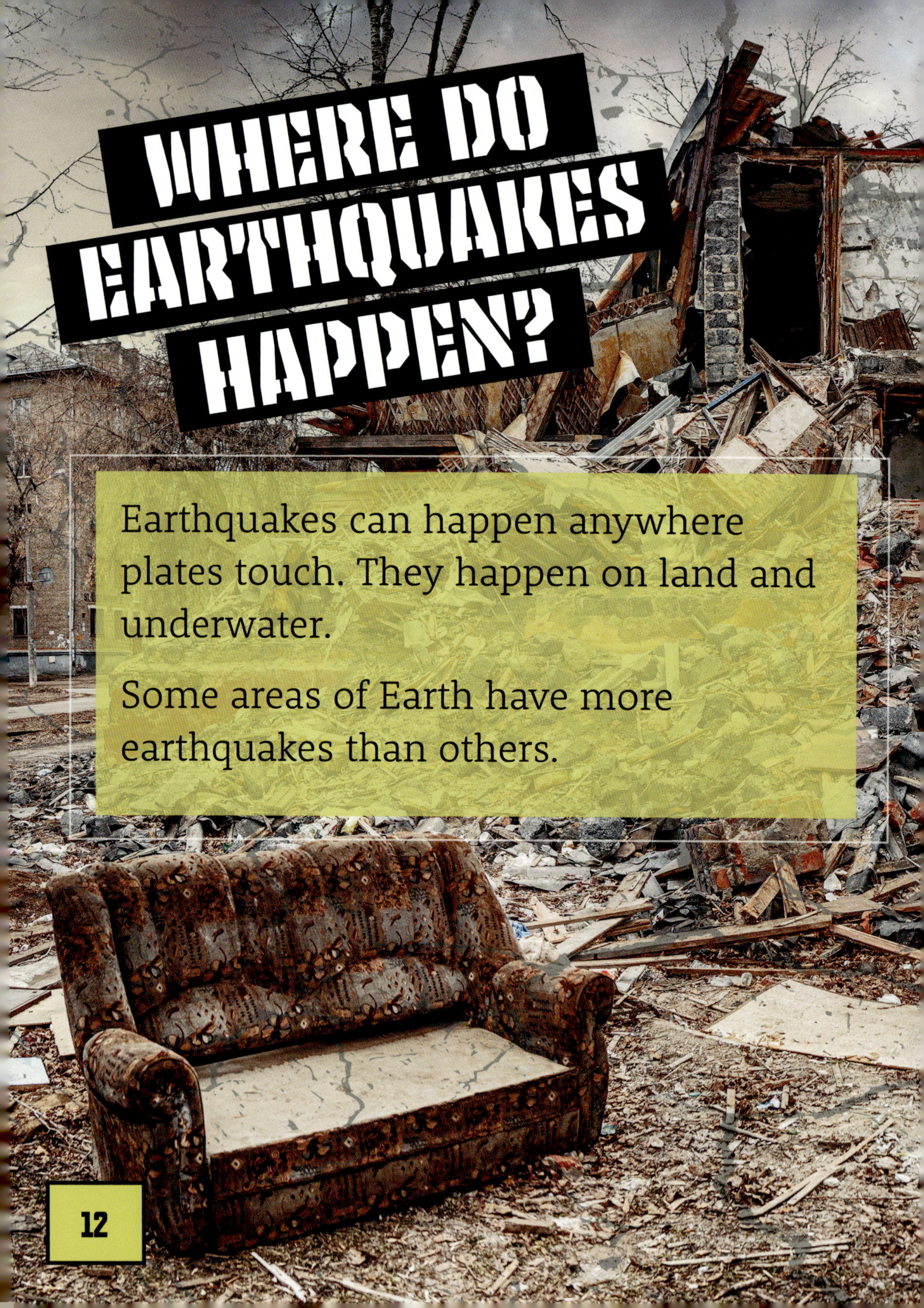

WHERE DO EARTHQUAKES HAPPEN?

Earthquakes can happen anywhere plates touch. They happen on land and underwater.

Some areas of Earth have more earthquakes than others.

The Pacific Plate bumps against other plates along the rim of the Pacific Ocean. About 81 percent of the world's largest earthquakes happen in this area.

WHY ARE EARTHQUAKES DANGEROUS?

Not all earthquakes are strong. Some **tremors** do little or no damage.

But a large earthquake's shaking can collapse buildings, roads, and bridges.

Gas and power lines may break and start fires.

Underwater earthquakes can trigger massive waves called **tsunamis**. A tsunami destroys anything in its path.

QUAKE FACT

Earthquakes can cause landslides. The ground's motion sends soil and rock tumbling down slopes, over roads, and into buildings.

THE WORLD'S DEADLIEST EARTHQUAKE

An earthquake struck China's Shaanxi Province in 1556.

It happened in a crowded area where many people lived in poorly built homes.

It is thought that up to 830,000 people died.

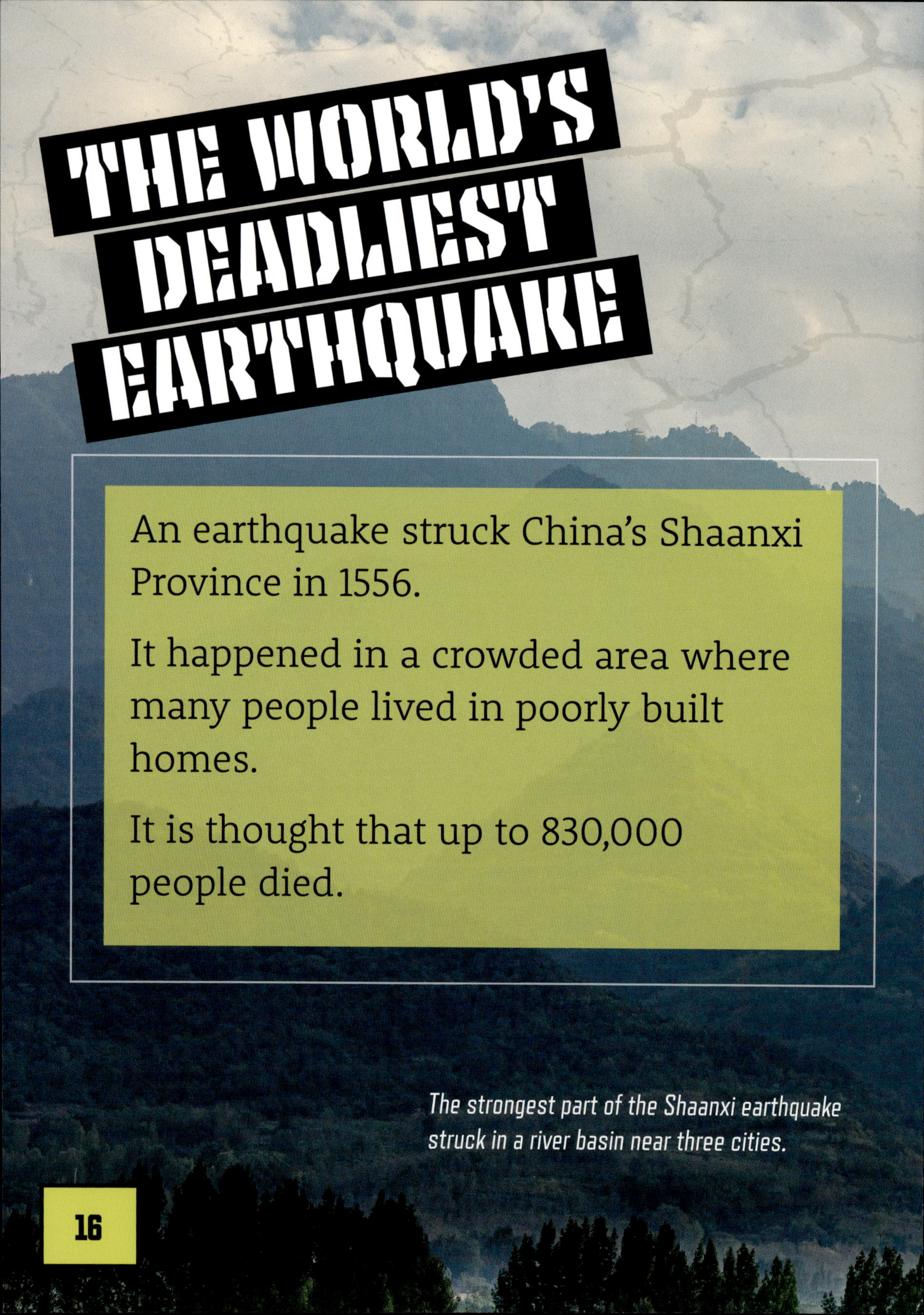

The strongest part of the Shaanxi earthquake struck in a river basin near three cities.

QUAKE FACT

The Great San Francisco Earthquake was one of the deadliest in United States history. A quake struck the city in 1906 and a fire followed. About 3,000 people died.

PREDICTING AN EARTHQUAKE

Scientists can't predict exactly where or when an earthquake will occur.

But some countries use earthquake early warning systems.

These systems **detect** ground motion as soon as an earthquake begins. An alert goes out.

The alert gives people a little time to prepare.

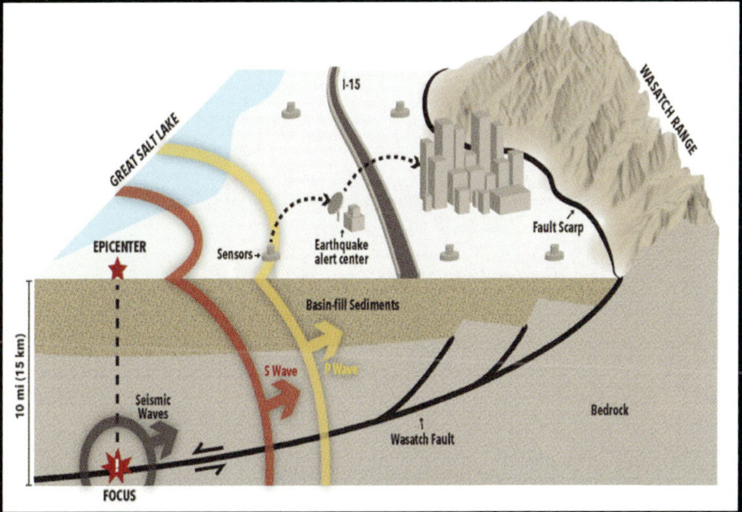

Sensors monitor the **seismic waves** deep inside Earth that happen during earthquakes.

STAYING SAFE DURING AN EARTHQUAKE

Do not run outside if you are indoors. It's safer to stay where you are.

Drop to your hands and knees. Crawl under a table or desk and hold on until the earthquake stops.

If you are outside, stay there and move away from power lines and buildings.

DROP
COVER
HOLD

GLOSSARY

crust (kruhst): the outermost shell of a planet

detect (di-TEKT): to discover the presence of something

faults (fawltz): cracks or a zone of cracks between two blocks of rock

plates (playtz): sections of Earth's crust

pressure (PRESH-ur): the force or weight produced when something pushes against something else

seismic waves (SIZE-mic wayvz): bursts of energy that move through the layers of Earth as a result of earthquakes, volcanic activity, large movements in the materials that make up the planet, and large man-made explosions

tremors (TREM-urz): minor shaking movements in the ground

tsunamis (tsu-NAH-meez): large, destructive ocean waves usually caused by underwater earthquakes

INDEX

AFTER READING QUESTIONS

1. What is a plate?
2. What happens along faults?
3. Why do many large earthquakes happen along the rim of the Pacific Ocean?
4. What kinds of damage can earthquakes cause?
5. How do early warning systems work?

About the Author

Tracy Vonder Brink loves true stories and facts. She has written more than twenty books for kids and is a contributing editor for three children's science magazines. Tracy lives in Cincinnati, Ohio, with her husband, two daughters, and two rescue dogs.

Written by: Tracy Vonder Brink
Design by: Under the Oaks Media
Editor: Kim Thompson

Photographs/Shutterstock: Tada Images: cover(top); 4.murat: cover(bottom); Fotos593: p. 4-5; FlyandDive: p. 5; YegoroV: p. 7; Vastram: p. 8-9; Adwo: p. 10-11; frantic00: p. 12-13; Ramazan Nacar: p. 14-15; Nelson Antoine: p. 15; Jun Yang: p. 16-17; Chadwick: p. 17; Christopher E Brown: p. 18-19; David Pereiras: p. 21

Library of Congress PCN Data
Earthquakes / Tracy Vonder Brink
Natural Disasters Where I Live
ISBN 978-1-63897-477-2(hard cover)
ISBN 978-1-63897-592-2(paperback)
ISBN 978-1-63897-707-0(EPUB)
ISBN 978-1-63897-822-0(eBook)
Library of Congress Control Number: 2021953377

Printed in the United States of America.

Seahorse Publishing Company
www.seahorsepub.com

Published in the United States
Seahorse Publishing
PO Box 771325
Coral Springs, FL 33077

SEAHORSE PUBLISHING